YOUR INVITATION TO A MODEST BREAKFAST

Published in the United States by Fence Books, Science Library 320, University at
Albany, 1400 Washington Avenue, Albany, NY 12222, www.fenceportal.org

Fence Books is a project of Fence Magazine, Incorporated, which is funded in
part by support from the New York State Council on the Arts and the National
Endowment for the Arts, along with the generous sponsorship of the New York
State Writers Institute and the University at Albany. Many thanks to these friends
and to all Friends of Fence.

Fence Books are distributed by Consortium Book Sales & Distribution (cbsd.com)
and Small Press Distribution (spdbooks.org)

and printed in Canada by The Prolific Group. (prolific.ca)

Cover and interior design by Victoria Pater

Library of Congress Cataloguing in Publication Data
Gamble, Hannah
Your Invitation to A Modest Breakfast/ Hannah Gamble

Library of Congress Control Number: 2012950436

ISBN 13: 978-1-934200-62-9

FIRST EDITION
10 9 8 7 6 5 4 3 2

YOUR INVITATION TO A MODEST BREAKFAST

HANNAH GAMBLE
2012 NATIONAL POETRY SERIES
SELECTED BY BERNADETTE MAYER

FENCE BOOKS
ALBANY NEW
YORK

THE NATIONAL POETRY SERIES

The National Poetry Series was established in 1978 to ensure the publication of five poetry books annually through five participating publishers. Publication is funded by the Lannan Foundation; Stephen Graham; Joyce & Seward Johnson Foundation; Juliet Lea Hillman Simonds; The Poetry Foundation; Olafur Olafsson, Mr. & Mrs. Michael Newhouse; Jennifer Rubell; The New York Community Trust; Elizabeth Christopherson; and Aristides Georgantas.

2011 COMPETITION WINNERS

The Apothecary's Heir, by Julianne Buchsbaum of Lawrence, KS
Chosen by Lucie Brock-Broido, to be published by Penguin Books

Your Invitation to a Modest Breakfast, by Hannah Gamble of Chicago, IL
Chosen by Bernadette Mayer, to be published by Fence Books

Green Is for World, by Juliana Leslie of Santa Cruz, CA
Chosen by Ange Mlinko, to be published by Coffee House Press

Exit, Civilian, by Idra Novey of Brooklyn, NY
Chosen by Patricia Smith, to be published by University of Georgia Press

Maybe the Saddest Thing, by Marcus Wicker of Ann Arbor, MI
Chosen by D.A. Powell, to be published by HarperCollins Publishers

This book is dedicated to Lydia, Josiah, Daniel, and Jessi

CONTENTS

A play about absurdity is a play against absurdity.
— **Elie Wiesel** to **Samuel Beckett**

YOUR INVITATION TO A MODEST BREAKFAST

It's too cold to smoke outside, but if you come over,
I'll keep my hands to myself, or won't I.
I would like to tell you about the wall eaten up

by the climbing plant—it was so beautiful.
Various things have been happening to me,
all of them sexual. The man on the bus

took off his pants so I could see him better.
Another man said, "Ignore him darlin'.
Just sit on my lap." But I'm not one of those

who's hungriest in the morning,
unlike the man at the bakery
who eats egg after egg after egg.

Listen. Come over: the cold has already eaten
the summer. I need another pair of ears:
from the kitchen I can't tell if I'm hearing wind chimes

or some gray woman with failing arms
dropping a pan full of onions and potatoes.
                              This morning I need four hands—

two to wash the greens, one to lift a teakettle,
one to pour the milk. This morning, one little mouth
will not do. We could play a game

where we crouch on the tiles, two yellow dogs
drinking coffee from bowls. We could play a game
where we let the breakfast burn.

Outside there's a world where every love scene
begins with a man in a doorway;
he walks over to the woman and says "Open your mouth."

LIGHT EXCESSES

That's me: the woman sitting
in her house among
many light excesses.
This is winter.
This is a heap of lacking
and the mind's trash
becoming the need
for many fabric protections,
in a way that quilts alone
could never be. I climbed up
on the bed to see you,
and the light from the ceiling
and the dresser lit your face
like an apple orchard on the day
a farmer's favorite horse
rose from the dead.

I AM TOLD A THING OR TWO ABOUT THE DUENDE

Admire the ballerina's throat first, get it out of the way. Admire the
workhorse capacity of her lungs, then ask her to take off her shoes
so you can see her toes black with ramming themselves again and
again into wood, into satin, into wood. She carries a beautiful death
in her lungs.

The gypsy plays best when the ashes from his first wife's clothes
blow into creaking folds of his accordion. One of her hairs still
tangled in the tambourine. His song flies past his rotting teeth with
the hope of comforting everyone he knows who is hungry, which is
everyone. His smoke-wife fills his lungs.

God is greeted at the edge of the forest with thanks for the pain
we felt while being alive—the lips we bit through, the knees in
our stomachs, the bones broken in the midst of doing something
wonderful, the ability to damage our bodies with enthusiasm. Our
fingertips brushed the feathered tail of "more," then our hearts gave
out; we fell onto our deflated lungs.

The Angel will just as soon put the flaming coal on another's
lips. The Muse will be happy to give your one remaining visit to
someone else. They both keep their distance. They detest your
sweat, they will be embarrassed if you cry out, if you begin to pace,
or talk to yourself. Only the Duende will [depending on his mood]
teach you to pray in Russian, offer you moonshine, stick his tongue
in your ear, or clamp his mouth over your own, sending his thick
cello-voice into your lungs.

If these dark sounds live in a woman, she will have eyes that want to splash out and baptize your face in dark water. Her hair will pull on its own roots, stretching out towards passersby because it wants to grow into them like vines. The Duende in the mouth of a woman sounds like the moan of a bull with a ribboned spear through its heart, ocean water bubbling in a child's lungs.

ANOTHER ROOM

When I was born, Mercy was there.
Slick and shrieking,
I felt ill-equipped.

When I asked to be sucked back
into the rumbling storm cloud
of the not-yet-born, it was Mercy
who shook her head.

She was there for my parents
and not for me.

Not until my fifteenth birthday,
and I barely remember
what happened that day—

A torn knee. A copperhead.
A neighbor's magazine
in the trashcan.
Skin imperfections
on the women we saw there,
and how they troubled us.

I was playing cards alone that night,
when Mercy came. *Take these keys,*
she said. My father's car
asleep in the driveway.
You can go away,
if not back to.

WE CAN WALK TOWARDS THE FUTURE AS TOWARDS A LUMINOUS CITY

Sustain yourself
with conversations
no one else is using.

Watch documentaries
about exceptional children,
and eat some animal protein.

Dress yourself in the dark.

Undress yourself
when he's out
getting the mail.

Strength is one goal,
and not tripping on the way up
the stairs is another.

Celebrate finishing
the things you begin.
Celebrate harder.

If the world feels like
it will shake you,
wear your puffy windbreaker
indoors. Now a stranger
could bump you in a doorway
and you might not even feel it.

Go through your receipts,
and you'll learn who you are.

If someone you know
asks you who *you* are
you can say nothing
and put on
your sunglasses.

Instead of doing your laundry,
put your quarters
in a gumball machine.

Instead of calling her,
sleep.

Instead of lying,
just tell him
something else.

I HAVE A RIGHT TO MY PREFERENCES

and may present them, if itemized,
before the Board of Directors. I know
that part of being human
is deferring to the experts.
If I was not supervised by a parental
bureaucracy, you would lose me
to the opium dens.
For I have heard that the philosophy
of the East is a more peaceful one.
Yet in the West it's said, if our lives
were meant to be peaceful, why did the Lord
give us fingernails to chew on?
With our teeth, humans are allowed only
to resolve intrapersonal conflicts,
and I'm thankful for it. My conflicts
with myself keep me from flying
in the face of strangers in the street,
unlike the man in Kafka's story, who would
snatch a woman's handbag on a crowded train,
rather than go home to his wife's face,
to which he was indifferent.

FOR I WILL CONSIDER MY HOUSEPLANT MAGDA

— After Christopher Smart

For I will consider my houseplant Magda
for she is not the servant of the living God
for she has no ears to hear him.

For if she sways her stalk of shining hairs
she does it to tempt, and not to praise.

For if she has grown taller
it is because she stood by the window
and not because someone told her to.

For if she has dirty feet
it is because I planned it that way.

For if she has no love for me
it is because I plucked a leaf
to shred in my worries.

For if she turns yellow
she does not deserve my attention.

For if I do not like yellow it is because
I never had a dress of that color.

For if I wore dresses
I would choose them in pinks
and apples, the colors with which
the Lord did not garnish Magda.

For if Magda glowed with roses
she would never be free of her lovers.

For even if her plant lovers left her alone
human lovers would pilfer her.

For no human can resist
a bud lit up by sunlight.

For it is in sunlight that I first
learned what I look like.

For if I did not know my face
I would see myself everywhere.

For an infant cannot tell that she is separate
from anyone who smells of milk.

For if the smell of milk does not lead to the taste
the mind will learn about identity.

For to know herself is a burden
that Magda will not have to bear.

For she does not listen to my interpretations
of her leaves and personality.

For she has tried to tell me a thing or two
but I do not want my thoughts contaminated by a pagan.

For Magda often exalts the sun with her body
and I rush to close the shutter with my dirty hand.

LEISURE, HANNAH, DOES NOT AGREE WITH YOU

— After Catullus

Leisure, Hannah, does not agree with you.
Mouth stuffed with garlic cloves
testicular in shape and pungency, you asked yourself permission
for a chicken's breast, a loaf of bread slicked with butter,
a cake with cherry glazes that would delight
any little girl with gaps in her teeth clapping "Cake!
Oh, cake! It is so worth a soiled dress!"
It's as if, Hannah, leisure entered through your pores
and made you poor in spirit: "I have no work to push me,
I have no love to hold me, I have no hope to lift me. Only cleaning—"
which is not truly leisure, Hannah!
But you can fold these shirts like they do in the boutiques, sweetness.
Take a little pride in the smallish things—how shiny, your blue teakettle!
Branches slam against the windows, but your house
is a fortress; and you are too, Hannah.

LEISURE, HANNAH, DOES NOT AGREE WITH YOU (2)

— After Catullus

My house disgusted me, so I slept in a tent.
My tent disgusted me, so I slept in the grass. The grass disgusted me,
so I slept in my body, which I strung like a hammock from two ropes.
My body disgusted me, so I carved myself out of it.

My use of knives disgusted me because it was an act of violence.
My weakness disgusted me because "Hannah" means "hammer."
The meaning of my name disgusted me because I'd rather be known
as beautiful. My vanity disgusted me because I am a scholar.

My scholarship disgusted me because knowledge is empty.
My emptiness disgusted me because I wanted to be whole.
My wholeness would have disgusted me because to be whole
is to be smug. Still, I tried to understand wholeness

as the inclusiveness of all activities: I walked out into the yard,
trying to vomit and drink milk simultaneously. I tried to sleep
while smoking a cigar. I have enough regrets to crack all the plumbing.
I'm whole only in that I've built my person from every thought I've ever loved.

WAITING UP

you have a cut above your right eye
where have you been

while you were gone none of our appliances
would work for me

none of the mirrors would talk
to me, either

I looked out the window and saw a tree
doubled over as if

its sap had suddenly curdled and I
was worried

if these sparse woods, if these faint vines
fall apart, isn't it because I'm

losing my hair, because I'm tearing my nails
away from my hands and you

came home tonight with a cut
and buttons missing

who is sending us this message
the paperboy

no longer comes to the house, maybe his bicycle
has rusted, maybe

a cancer took both of his legs
why did you

come home tonight if you aren't
ready to tell me

WE HAVE NO INSTINCTS, ONLY LEGS TO RUN ON

and when one is running, all objects
appear blurry. I do not understand
how I see some movements of your face,

and not others. I know
that with each flinch you are telling me
something. I have forgotten what to ask

because now there is nothing but
questions. In an ocean, I can't see
the drops of water and also,

not the salt. Once you described
my temperament as salty, and not
in a kind way. Similarly,

my nose is longer than yours
and I never knew to feel bad
about it. For I was born innocent

and stayed that way until only
recently. So I define innocence
in my own way and refuse to listen

to people who pay no attention
to how I like to be spoken to. I learned
to be demanding from the Lord, who asks

a lot of me. If I disappoint him, it is only
because at night, I'm too tired. It is at night
that the Lord wants my courage,

and he brings his creations to my door
to test me. I send them away
with words, but often I fear

that they will send *me away*
and live in my house where it's warmer,
since the human home is the envy

of creation. We use our homes to advertise
our blessings. Yet creation does not feel blessed
and someone told me that's our fault.

BIOTIC/ ABIOTIC

This is the movement
a poem makes: a trash bag
breaking and breaking
until a brilliant red pear
falls out, whole and un–
troubled—*how did that
happen?* You moved around
me like a plastic daisy
on a plastic stem, spinning
in yardwind. We never really
got it together. I think you prefer
astronomy because how far away
everything is is exactly
the order of things. I prefer poems,
but I understand that their human smell
is often troubling. The lack of this
is another good thing
about a star's dying, I guess.

OPENING REMARKS FOR OCTOBER

Welcome to the first October
of our household's undoing.
So many objects to say
goodbye to. You'll recall September,
when I took off my shoes
and was glad for it—
only sometimes
are tearful goodbyes appropriate.
Like when I took your body
off of my daily usage body.
There was the sound
of ice, spittle, redwoods.
Often I'm unsure
about propriety: The sounds
we made goodbying
seemed like the right ones,
but who can tell in this light.

2

IN A TIME OF WAR

That was the period when our daughter
would come crying into our bedroom
whenever the grackles began mating on the roof.
It isn't hurting them, my wife would say,

birds have tiny penises. Then two cats would
find their way into our bushes and start howling
like their skin was being peeled off. Oh, our daughter
with the endless tears. I brought my wife wine

every night for a week, hoping I'd arrange for us a son.
The cats aren't killing each other, sweetness,
said my wife's purple lips, *it's just that all male cats,*
not just the wild ones, have barbs on their penises.

What what what, sobbed my daughter, *is a penis?*
A son, a son, a son, I thought, as I held my wife
at the hips, on the floor to avoid hitting
the wall with our bed; our daughter had cried herself

into unconsciousness, and maybe I was sure
she wouldn't hear when I yelled my way farther
into my wife, my mouth still in a "son" shape.
Our daughter woke herself up with a howl

she didn't know the reason for, and my wife
turned back at me with several reasons to scowl
texturing her red face. We were covered
when our daughter came in, tears and snot

curling her hair against her cheeks. *It's ok, lovely,*
my wife said. *I was just on the floor looking*
for something and I was caught by a tiny barb.
I took it out, and now I'm going to go to sleep.

THE BIRTHDAY

When I was born my mother presented me
to my father in a box. His fingers tangled
in the wrapping only to hang still at the sight
of my dark hair. I had no teeth, but was already

scanning the horizon for people to eat, clouds
to inhale, for leaves to rub against my skin
until my soft, folded elbows were bright
green in the scent of lemons and limes

that would live in the curls of my ears, if I ate
the right kinds of leaves, only the bright green leaves.
My father could not appreciate my appetite,
for he was now tearing at the shoulders

of my mother's nightgown crying, "But what's it for?"
finally running out of the room, swinging me by
a pinkish ankle. My mother sighed
at the exhausted midwife, who was white

as a broken almond in the presence of such a man.
Downstairs, such a man was thrusting handfuls
of coffee into my pale shell gums, saying "Grind!"
then pressing my small, slick body onto the window glass,

saying "Shade!", then setting the phonograph needle
on my intricate thumbprint, saying "Play!"
and waiting for all my goodness and blessings
to be apparent, waiting for a devoted kiss.

EVERYTHING THAT'S ALIVE STAYS THAT WAY

The war was everywhere, not just in the desert
where we expected it to be.
One night I heard the war in the wall behind my head—
an animal with thick skin-wings
beating another toothy beast, claws hitting fur, wood, flesh.
I asked my neighbor later
what it had been like to be alive before a time of war,
and he said it was funny
we even have a word for it, because everything
that's alive stays that way
by tearing heat from another's belly.

THE THING I WAS HOLDING

No thing but the thing I was holding.
The sound of a vacuum in the air.
A fruit fly dipping like a piece of ash.

The housekeeper was there,
vacuuming for my mother,
who had had a fifth child.

I climbed up the lilac tree,
but not to have a look around.
Fearing the sound of the vacuum,
I was a toothy child
and a shaky animal.

My father slept in the day
till the vacuum woke him.
He wound his sweater
around his head. He went out
on the porch to take a look around
and saw the lilac tree.
He imagined the Lions of God
were guarding it. He imagined
a woman running the vacuum
and all of his thoughts
being sucked from the carpet.

Part beast in the lilac tree,
I hid from the mailman
and from others.

My father often promised,
"Tomorrow I will rise early
and will not your sweetness offend,"
so I know how to stay away
from those who make promises.

I love my friends dearest
who make only premises.
"Hannah holds her own hand
at the top of a lilac tree"
is one premise I like so dearly.

SUNDAYS

Boys pressing their shirts because mothers.
            All I ever wanted
      was no cruelty.

           Now the brain become a dish
               that sorry eats up.

I've put three gashes in my side—
           out comes oil, milk, more oil.
      I need no clothes.

Sleep
will be my river.

The earth, it makes a mighty smell.
People:
        sweet and funny
        rotting things.

I have to love

those rotting things;
           look at mirrors, windows, ponds,
          saying *Hannah,*
              you're a scooped-up animal.

Rescue,
here I come.

      But where can go
my little shoes,

crying like a choke
on something?

Shut up, snotty babies,
                    Hannah needs her heart fall out
and sleep under some cold rock/ tree.

HOW EARLY TO WAKE

—After Mary Ruefle

All my life I felt a heavy hand
pushing some thoughts out
through the plushy curtains
of this or that opera house
and holding others back
with a shepherd's crook
or a firm look that says
Quiet. Still, I was grateful
that I had decided some thoughts
are worth the water and snackpacks
it takes to keep them alive.
When I watched television
I saw other people's decisions
in motion: This one decides to keep
her baby; that one decides he will never again
leave his home. Even when I was not being
a poet, I was deciding how early to wake—
how early to begin the business of approving
and disapproving of the shapes
I'd let my person take.

LETTER FROM THERE

Well, my feet had dirt on them
pretty much all of the time.
Because it was my birthday,
I was given a piñata and I beat it
very thoroughly. Sobbing all the while,
I told my dearest friend
she would never be happy. *This is not
my wish for you,* I said, *I am not trying
to issue a curse.* (But what *should* we do
with the thoughts when we think them?)
I found exercise to be very useful.
I found books to be a knife
and a comfort. But confronted on the road
by many automobiles, I was indecent
and abandoned my kindness.
What can you spare? Asked a man
dressed in Christmas, and I said
Only the things I dislike, and handed him
the hardest peach from my bag.

I WAS BUSY

That was the year that my brother put dates (2/17/04) on everything:
the mirror (12/3/04), the tea-bag tags (3/8/04, 10/9/04, 1/30/04),
and the dog's water bowl (9/25/04). *I'm alive right now, and have*

been for a while, was what he told me. He insisted that his meals of
pork BBQ were not inconsequential. He had noticed that when
babies crawled out from women's dresses, everyone

cried and took pictures. He said he was thankful for our scrapbook
minds: How "Pizza lunch with Uncle Albert" shares a ribboned
corner with "Jessica marries a man with a crooked bow tie." But I

was busy noticing how fat girls hide their bellies behind notebooks
and couch cushions. Isn't everything cruel?

COCKTAIL PARTY

The last time I saw my father alive
he was on his way to a cocktail party, wearing a tie
that was much too business-like for a cocktail party,

just like the first time he went to a Rock & Roll concert,
and his mother made him wear a three-piece suit.

He was carrying a deep blue pot full of stew, and I said
Didn't you say this was a cocktail party? And he said
I don't think anyone would say no to free stew. So I helped him

strap the large pot into the passenger's seat of his car,
while his date, a thin woman from his office, climbed
into the back with her shawl.

I stayed in that night, and washed the dishes
from dinner, his salad of cheeses and mandarin oranges.

I got the call next morning. The thin woman's shawl
had been stolen and my father had stepped
onto a fire truck moments before it raced
to a fire. He was presumed dead, but one young man

had seen him, carrying armfuls of potted plants
from the burning building which, with the sounds
of dogs and women howling, appeared to be levitating.

THE STORIES I TELL DO NOT HAVE ENDINGS

because clouds, deserts, and viruses do not end,
nor do they understand that all we humans can do
is squeal in our kitchens at the sight of the real survivors,
the cockroaches which can live for three years on a raisin.
Time for them goes so slowly. "And for me also,"
 said my grandmother, who was tired of us all.

"We're sorry," we often said to her face and body, buried
with her back to us under an afghan
(though a teacher once told me that women should never
apologize, and that weakness wears a kind face).

Once I thought I wanted to be a peacemaker,
but then I saw I hadn't thought things through
well enough. For I love how a sharp word cuts its way
from my mouth, and the peacemakers do not get to sweat enough!

A cry of anger resembles the cry of love, and vice versa.
(See how I'm using Latin to compensate for my lack
of democratic civility? See how I use the rhythms
of multisyllabics to calm my hissing nerves?)

When she died, my grandmother's nerves shrieked
and jumped toward me like fleas.
My birthright is a painted doll
and a stomach full of night crawlers.

I shouldn't feel so unwelcomed here! The world should see
that I'm one of her own!

And if I were to have a child
it would be only because I want to study
the same person for eighteen years. For I'm never able
to get to know someone
before they get up and interrupt my note-taking.
But without notes, I would forget these words
and would have to shriek and howl in my fur,
and then the peacemakers would approach me.

SUMMER IN THE FIRST DAYS

Mint is exquisite
    and a poem is a thing
that keeps me from moving around.

Writing a poem
      is wrapping a shining insect of the enchanted morning
    in cheesecloth
    and enjoying the urgent and tiny
      flashes of purple.

    Everything I want to tell you
would make a wonderful sound
hitting your windowpane,

but words
      aren't a natural thing.

There was the time I bound my arms
    and then tried to hold out my hands,
    and then was sad when
I couldn't hold out my hands.

What is love, we ask,
and the woman
    on the telephone says,
Oh, nothing much,
I just got back from the store.

CASA GRANDE

At the Casa Grande disco, men hold on
to other men's behinds, and women
hold on to men's behinds,
and everyone is holding on
to what it means to be dancing
and holding on, and I am there
too, doing the two things
I am always doing:
holding on, and drinking enough
water so that tomorrow I'll be able
to document all the things humans do
to endear themselves to me, conscious
of how the dancing
will bring them closer,
and take them farther away.

BY HIMSELF ON A SUNDAY,

a man has an orgasm

and feels anything is possible.

In his mind
he is rowing on a pond,
throwing his body back and forth
to get to a bell tower
where his name is engraved
on the bell's inner lip,
in a lighter, cleaner gold.

The man is picturing a girl
walking home,
wearing boots that black tea
smells like.

He pictures her on a bed,
taking off the boots.

> Evening birds
> are making the sounds
> of October cooling.

He understands the way
she holds
her own breast as she sleeps.

EDITORS REMOVE THE SKELETAL OLD WOMEN
FROM THE GUSTAV KLIMT PAINTINGS THAT APPEAR IN BOOKS AND CALENDARS

I fear those people
who want love when I don't want to give it,

like my landlady Mirta
            with her crepe paper face,

pleading and smiling with all her gingivitis at me.
I'm not her sweetest,

and I could never love a person so afraid of looters,
dogs, or the Middle East.
This morning I burned kale
to the pan   and now Mirta fears
Teflon poisoning.
It's easy for her to love me as her past

but hard for me to love her as my future.

When the hurricane came,
Mirta's ancient parents shuffled around the house
with cotton balls
and rubbing alcohol.   I wore my youth
like a glossy fur coat.

Even now, the hunchbacked two pad slowly in slippers,
following my smell.   I shake my head at them.
As I see it,

the old have understood something horrible·
and become theaters of bad news.

The young put them away.

A PRAYER FOR MIRTA

who buys Church's Chicken for dinner
and thus shows she has given up on life.

A prayer for Mirta who believes
that I am a thief
and sets her Tupperware on the table
to count them.

In all of Mirta's stories,
life is unkind
and television is horrible.

In all of Mirta's stories,
someone denies her basic worth,
and she considers making
a counterargument.

Beside a bureau of porcelain eggs,
Mirta is watching television,
and I am watching Mirta.

Mirta whose husband
beat her teeth into a row of pomegranate seeds.

Mirta alone on a Saturday.

Mirta whose children prefer their father.

Goddamn it.

For most of us, death is the first time
           our friends will lift us up
and carry us on their shoulders.

GROUP MEDITATION POST ALLISON

After the funeral we all took up hobbies. One of us would call
another of us and say *My cereal tastes funny does your cereal taste funny?*
and then we would all agree or disagree about whether the cereal
was poison from China and some of us had children with whom we were
increasingly humorless.
                    Don't even play with me, some of us would say.

Others of us would remain alone, alone, and would stand in our kitchens,
hungry after a long day of being alive and would not be eating,
but would instead be writing poems that had to be written: *Oh, Allison…*

I was trying to record all of this with my camera.

When Allison left she was attached to a string that now pulled
many of our faces down in new ways, *Oh Allison.*

One of us was baptized at the YMCA and was given a new name that Allison
would have laughed at. Another of us also inched closer to religion,
lining his bird's cage with scientology bulletins.

I don't see spots, I see pulsating stripes,
one of us said on the phone with another. *What does it mean
to not hear the alarm clock anymore?* I asked her.

It's 7:30, the one of us who was in bed with me
                            would sometimes helpfully say.

Those eggs are expired you won't want to eat those, I would say to the one of us
who could smell nothing but disinfectant these days.

I wrote in a letter that day
that we were not the body of Christ,

                     but we were some kind of body.

BATHTUB CAPABILITIES

It's time to let
the water hold you.

Celebrate the way
you kept it together—

even in the library,
where all the books you love

had been especially
loved by others—

especially handled,
and especially wrinkled,

subsequently; oh look,
outside a woman shakes water

from her umbrella.
She's in it. She's in it

with you. If you happen to
catch the same plane

together one day,
you can hold her face

in your sagging eyes' gaze
long enough for your face

to strike hers
as familiar.

MAYBE A FAREWELL TOUR

Because it had grown warmer in the night
I realized that while I was sleeping

your anger towards me
must have lessened.

Letters to my friends begin: "Writing you here,
among the poinsettias…"

and then I drop my pen
and think about how, at this moment,

my mother and her God are alone in a room,
and he is comforting her.

THINK ABOUT A KNOT OF TWINE

1. The knot of twine held my legs to my body.
   They met like the part of the tree where birds live.

2. It wasn't the knot of twine that held my breast
   to my back, instead it was my jacket.

3. Not everyone's knot of twine will look the same—
   some people want do things simply,
   and other people's insecurities prevent them.

4. Vonnegut would have tied a simple knot:
   "Any scientist who can't explain what he does
   to a seven year old is a charlatan."

5. Newton tied beautiful knots in the dark;
   He wrote in Latin so "common people" couldn't read it.

6. But canoes, cowboys, the recipient of a parcel—all of these
   appreciate a simple knot of twine.

7. Could we arrive at a place after walking there together—
   our two little fingers pulled together by a loop of twine?

8. In my mind the twine is yellow
   and you are throwing bread at my feet,
   surrounding me with a soft crowd of white ducks.

9. Mother, I said, leaving her body,
   my organs seem to be on the outside.
   They are tied to your body by a length of twine.

10. "Why can't we?" said some of us, noticing that the people, cities, and animals in the world were drifting apart.

"We can," said the length of twine, and it knotted itself.

RICHES

The café is indelicate.
            The café wears a filth that ensparkles it.
    The man with the beard   is rough
        as if stitched out of burlap. His two white ducks
are circling his feet, entwining their ribbons.

A clean woman stencils invitations—
        She's creating a party for all the full figured girls in catalogues.
To her party they will wear emeralds—
        as many   as their heavy haunches will support.

        Two men speaking over a table: *How are you feeling?*
                               Gentle.

God of the great world's sucking mouth,

I want to worship
        but all these riches catch my eye.

IT WAS ALIVE, THOUGH DIFFERENTLY

It had a secret name
which in later years came to mean
I will continue to stand here.

It had a food mouth
and a shrieking mouth.

Popular wisdom indicated
that Its hands could heat stones
and that a man could cook
meat on those stones.

That being said,
It had a poverty hand
and a riches hand.

They were
the same hand.

A little ways above the hands
the mouths spoke together
but for two
different reasons,
like the music was behaving
but the orchestra was broken.

★

Even in less
benevolent moments,
It was known to use Its own

body as a tent and as the gifts
inside of the tent.

Early people said It had a mother hand
and a father hand, and that together
they made a clapping sound.

Its hands delivered the children
from madness.

The hands saw the riverbank sliding
into the river
to make
a more shallow river.

They scooped the mud up.
The hands were giving thanks.

★

The hands smelled like exodus.
The hands were the law.

One hand grew older, and the other
hand younger.

They said, fairly often,
We'd like to try that again.

Both were restless
and wanted rest.

One hand said, *I will go where you go,*
while the other hand continued
on alone.

JOY BOX

Grandmother. Something has happened with factories,
  and with growth.
      With the West, and with traveling.
Seeing less of farms, and families,
  and staying on the same land, in the same town.
In my History class I wanted to talk about all of it
    and the professor said *"Growth,*
  just say *growth"*—

  So that's what's happened to us,
you and I; my feet have taken on
a big country and your feet
  get smaller and smaller while you slop your apartment
  a new shade of mauve;
you're knitting;
all the couches are covered in blankets, but it's still the same apartment
  you birthed my father in, the same apartment
    where you hit everyone
with your hairbrush.

  So now we don't know if it's age or the pills
    that moved your mind or your hand
when you wrote "Happy Birthday…"
and then covered the card with the words
  we read as "Joy Box," which we agreed referred to me,
and not to your home,
and not to a thing you carry inside of you,
because in your Christmas speech you said
  "I have nothing" and fell asleep.

Grandmother. Can you sense, across states,
        that I want you to turn the television off
and picture me in a place
where it's raining.   I remember that you are the land
       that grew the land
            that grew me,

       but then I left all your green,
and am now in a place where the land is so flat

that if I stand on the lawn, and you would just
       turn the TV off, I might be able to throw you something
                     you could
catch in your hand:
an apple, a tennis ball, a picture of my father smiling in your
sunglasses
next to his father, who wasn't looking at you,
            or my father, or the dog—he was staring out
past a smoking barbeque pit and saying
       A Mexican came into the store the other day
and I treated him like I treat everyone else.

       Grandmother, he never was kind
           until he had to cook for you—to open
cans of fifty cent chili and spread the margarine
        on crackers. It's because you've given up in that chair—
you don't even laugh
       at the dog anymore.   I think it will be next year
when someone calls my father to say that now,
       in the least disputable way,
           he no longer has a mother.

But until then, Grandmother,

I think of you
            on other grass.

NEIGHBORHOOD BEAUTIFICATION

Hello, poet. I read your book again today,
and with Houston finally being
what I want it to be (windy
and piled with the bodies of pumpkins)
I have to say I felt
alone. Alone is a proud
and quiet feeling where I am everything
and everything is a cluster of four pumpkin-colored
leaves on a tree still green in October.

There are several white berries
in the leaves where to live
in Houston is to hear the cries
of neighborhood beautification machines
which only sound human if my friends
are away. People say people are hard
to understand, but those people
aren't paying attention.

In Houston, I explore
the alleys of Chinatown alone.
Table cloths, flowers, and trash mean
someone is having a wedding.
Thanks to a sudden parade
of sirens, the nearby restaurant
won't burn after all; maybe after,
everyone will put on nicer clothes
and come celebrate the marriage.

The world will always burn and be
flooded with aid. In their colors, four leaves
in October are dying and celebrating.
I, myself, any one of us could say,
am a marriage.

ACKNOWLEDGEMENTS

Thanks to my teachers, Tony Hoagland, Matthew Zapruder, and Bruce Smith, who continue to be encouraging even in the absence of institutional obligation. You've changed the way I think about poems and teaching and life.

Thanks and love to Sean Bishop and Eric Ekstrand, kind people/ brilliant poets, for caring about me and my work. I am very lucky to have shared a city and writing program with you for 3 years.

Love and gratitude forever to my family, Mom, Dad, Lisa, Lydia, Josiah, Daniel, and Jessi.

Thanks to the University of Houston Creative Writing program/ English Department, especially j. Kastely, Tamara Fish, and all of the talented and insightful poets who helped with these poems. I really wasn't a poet before.

Thanks to the English faculty at Rice University for giving me a year (and an office in which) to make this book what it is. Thanks to the Edward F. Albee Foundation for the residency that gave me time and space to write, and to Inprint Inc. for the fellowship that helped me to afford graduate school.

A very big thank you to Rick Jackson who recruited me, very resistant at the time, into his poetry workshop and introduced me to contemporary poetry. You started everything, Rick.

Thanks to all the people who have gone out of their way to tell me that they like my poems.

Very big thank yous to Bernadette Mayer for choosing my book, to Rebecca Wolff for making these poems better with her edits and insight, and to Victoria Pater for making this book look amazing, inside and out. Beautiful ladies: thank you.

Thanks to all the editors who have been excited about my work. The following poems appeared in the following journals:

* *Barnstorm,* "I Have a Right to My Preferences"
* *Cimarron Review,* "Waiting Up"
* *Drunken Boat,* "How Early to Wake"
* *Ecotone,* "Your Invitation to a Modest Breakfast"
* *Forklift, Ohio,* "Cocktail Party"
* *Hayden's Ferry Review,* "I Am Told a Thing or Two about the Duende," published as "The Anima Talks to Paganini about the Duende"
* *Indiana Review,* "In a Time of War," "Light Excesses," "Bathtub Capabilities"
* *Ink Node,* "Everything That's Alive Stays That Way"
* *iO: A Journal of New American Poetry,* "Group Meditation Post Allison"
* *La Fovea,* "The Stories I Tell Do Not Have Endings"
* *Loaded Bicycle,* "Leisure, Hannah, Does Not Agree with You," "Leisure, Hannah, Does Not Agree with You (2)," "Think About a Knot of Twine"
* *Mid-American Review,* "For I Will Consider My Houseplant Magda"
* *Phantom Limb,* "I Was Busy"
* *Pinwheel,* "Neighborhood Beautification," "Summer in the First Days," "We Can Walk Towards the Future as Towards a Luminous City"
* *The Columbia Review,* "Letter from There"
* *Third Coast,* "The Birthday"

THE MOTHERWELL PRIZE

Negro League Baseball   Harmony Holiday
living must bury   Josie Sigler
Aim Straight at the Fountain and Press Vaporize   Elizabeth Marie Young
Unspoiled Air   Kaisa Ullsvik Miller

THE ALBERTA PRIZE

The Cow   Ariana Reines
Practice, Restraint   Laura Sims
A Magic Book   Sasha Steensen
Sky Girl   Rosemary Griggs
The Real Moon of Poetry and Other Poems   Tina Brown Celona
Zirconia   Chelsey Minnis

FENCE MODERN POETS SERIES

Eyelid Lick   Donald Dunbar
Nick Demske   Nick Demske
Duties of an English Foreign Secretary   Macgregor Card
Star in the Eye   James Shea
Structure of the Embryonic Rat Brain   Christopher Janke
The Stupefying Flashbulbs   Daniel Brenner
Povel   Geraldine Kim
The Opening Question   Prageeta Sharma
Apprehend   Elizabeth Robinson
The Red Bird   Joyelle McSweeney

NATIONAL POETRY SERIES

Your Invitation to a Modest Breakfast   Hannah Gamble
A Map Predetermined and Chance   Laura Wetherington
The Network   Jena Osman
The Black Automaton   Douglas Kearney
Collapsible Poetics Theater   Rodrigo Toscano

ANTHOLOGIES & CRITICAL WORKS

Not for Mothers Only: Contemporary Poets on Child-Getting & Child-Rearing
– Catherine Wagner & Rebecca Wolff, editors

A Best of Fence: *The First Nine Years,* Volumes 1 & 2
— Rebecca Wolff and Fence Editors, editors

POETRY

FICTION

 has a mission to redefine the terms of accessibility by publishing challenging writing distinguished by idiosyncrasy and intelligence rather than by allegiance with camps, schools, or cliques. It is part of our press's mission to support writers who might otherwise have difficulty being recognized because their work doesn't answer to either the mainstream or to recognizable modes of experimentation.

For information about our book prizes, or about *Fence*, visit www.fenceportal.org.